Case Memory

Stefania Irene Marthakis

SPUYTEN DUYVIL
New York City

Acknowledgements

Versions of some of these poems appeared in the following publications: *Bombay Gin, Small Town, Pinstripe Fedora, Lungfull!, The Accompanist,* and a broadside from *Farfalla Press*.

This collection of poems began during my time at Naropa University. With gratitude for their mentorship: Bhanu Kapil, Eleni Sikelianos, Reed Bye, Anne Waldman, and in memory of Anselm Hollo and Akilah Oliver. Onward.

Thank you to Jessica Rogers-Cerrato for creative guidance and support of this book throughout the years.

And with thanks to Megan London, and the editors at Spuyten Duyvil publishing.

"A purple room" poem is in memory of my great-grandmother Irene G. Paszkiewicz.

© 2021 Stefania Irene Marthakis
ISBN 978-1-956005-16-5

Library of Congress Cataloging-in-Publication Data

Names: Marthakis, Stefania Irene, author.
Title: Case memory / Stefania Irene Marthakis.
Description: New York City : Spuyten Duyvil, [2021] |
Identifiers: LCCN 2021036104 | ISBN 9781956005165 (paperback)
Subjects: LCGFT: Poetry.
Classification: LCC PS3613.A777754 C37 2021 | DDC 811/.6--dc23
LC record available at https://lccn.loc.gov/2021036104

The intoxicating poetics of Stefania Irene Marthakis' *Case Memory* explore the surreality of the quotidian, vividly portrayed here in an uncanny documentary form. Readers are invited to step into the screen/text, as the Prologue notes, we are the "passengers [who] arrive and leave at no set time." Marthakis uses a cinematic lens to explore the ways in which outside perceptions shape the narrator's (and our) understanding of society and self. Characters are defined by how they are perceived: Cast of Laughables, Even Number of Sentences, Girl in Drag, Charlie born with wings. Emotions grow unchecked and become characters themselves capable of keeping their own secrets. Diction fractures, reassembles, shatters, and reforms. As we are pulled deeper into the scenery, lights flicker, the windows are covered and uncovered with garbage bags, while an uneasy yet seductive tension simmers beneath the daily routine. *Case Memory* is a hauntingly beautiful work that invites readers to question the "positions [we] were assigned years ago." The Epilogue here is a gift, reminding us that uncertainty means nothing is set in stone and in each new circumstance we are "waking up to arrive again."
—Jessica Rogers-Cerrato, Writer & Archivist

To step in is to breathe deep and hold, a disruption, so fluid its cuts seamlessly transposable, at once structure and infrastructure, character and flaw, scene and unseen, always at the surface some relevant thing not to be forgotten for how it takes an other form, a new name, a time stamp—the continuum not a line but a thread, needling into focus so sharp you shield your eyes to save your lungs.
—Megan London, poet and editor of transient/vanity press

Stefania Irene Marthakis's *Case Memory* weaves intricate mysteries in a world where everything is animate, life is theater, and the pretend is truth. Dazzling prose poems, dialogue between unique characters, surreal snapshots, and lyrical beauty evoke a sense of wonder.
—Lisa Panepinto, author of *where i come from the fish have souls*

in memory of my grandfather Walter M. Matusik

PROLOGUE

ACT I: ENERGY MEETS RESISTANCE

ACT II: THE MAKING OF A JURY

ACT III: STATION 30: AN EMERGENCY POST

EPILOGUE

CASE MEMORY

Prologue

There is a wood floor, three movable walls held up by rusty wires, a box in the middle not taped shut shutters overlapping and tucked. There is a single light bulb that never stays in one place. An unmarked stage, an audience circumstantial, a Cast of Laughables, multiple rooms, and space with questionable safety. Memories and dreams play out on a film screen upstage. A train stops behind where an audience would sit. Passengers arrive and leave at no set time. There is no set weather schedule. What is in the box is not as important as why it is there. The original contents were model airplanes, assembly required. Sounds repeat until they become actions. There is a performance waiting for water. Lighting, no set time. A figure appears. Penny Detective sits in the audience, unties red scarf from eyes. Even Number of Sentences brings a jar with a set of teeth floating in it from backstage. Penny Detective places teeth in mouth. Positions were assigned years ago. Curtain up. There is shaking.

Act I:
Energy Meets Resistance

Girl in Drag wakes up in the Always Room. Girl in Drag spends the day with the alphabet, dwelling on a first-round-out spelling bee contestant. Newspaper reads Child Missing After Losing Spelling Bee. The picture of the girl's walk off stage captivates her.

Shake at slowness. Speak only when there is no expectation. No note only pictures. Charts and grids are designed. What if is applied. Would the contestant's family never speak the word *diphtheria* again? Habits, of course, are well known to be card sharks. Hints are in the cabinets.

In this business of selling eggs, Three Women sometimes Four are pitching their Jesus, Mary, and Josephs. Girl in Drag does not respond quickly enough. A phone call is placed. The Agreeable Utensil is handed down.

How could a girl accept? She already has a Depressed Refrigerator. They are seen often having drinks together, drawing boxes, and debating the social conditions of red polite.

The culprit is an angry, apple-eyed girl, a nickname from the second grade. Her grandfather says she is a possible flower. Play simple. Clean shaven necks, the smell of a Sharpie marker, and orange peel underneath fingernails. This is a room only in the head. Shh, the listeners will not tell. Gather and leave evidence to take a lifetime. A small tape recorder comes in handy. A train horn, a steel mill, this is home.

All the windows are covered with garbage bags. Duct tape secure.

Light cannot keep quiet. Visitors are a surprise. Strawberry milk.

She is in search of a description, a place, a questionnaire of very ables.

Three Women sometimes Four: A girl in drag in a room, a girl drags
a girl in a room, a drag in a girl room.

Entertain a punch as if it is Tuesday and there is nothing to fear. Immediate thank-you is necessary after the first couple bites.

Girl in Drag remembers a shopping mall and a high school swimming pool.

Toss at a wall, theater terrorism and no decisions, very drunk indeed.

Boy with many Occupations leaves the projector on again.

Set definitions to rummage. Fill shoes with a Penny Detective.

She reads a chapter from In the Service of Violence Against Herself.

Can make perfectly calm shadows misbehave. The ankles heal quite nicely. The language daughters are named, put away, and marked piano day. Mirror has its own ideas.

She leans out the window and screams airplanes for Charlie.

The Cast of Laughables prepares the witnesses.

Slack must be provided to prevent the film from tearing.

> *It is evening*
> *in the Always Room.*
> Predictions depend on counting.

Lighting contrast ratio is the ratio of key plus fill lights to fill light alone (K+F:F).

> Right foot down first.
> Circle bed twice.
> Secure ribbons around ankles.
> To justify is to practice.

The joining of two shots, with the abrupt ending of one shot and the immediate beginning of the next, is called a cut.

> Place an ad for
> soft typewriter.
> Await response.
> Read instructions
> on instructional reading.

The swish pan, a fast pan that blurs everything between the beginning and end of the movement.

> Get anger over
> tea-stained cups and
> must-say compliments.
> Memorize sitcom gestures,
> it will come in handy.

f-stop=<u>focal length</u>
   lens diameter

    Hungry but read delivery menu
    instead to subside the needing.
    Somewhere someone
    plays go fish
    and chances the farm.

Soft light is a large, scoop-shaped fixture that blocks all direct light from the bulb so that only bounced light escapes.

    Today is not safe
    for skipping.
    Play with even numbers.
    Go to sleep.

Evidence finds neighbors. A boy named Charlie born with wings. They are removed to ensure a normal childhood.

He draws airplanes and birds.

Ways he dreams of speaking.

He tapes them on the window for Girl in Drag.

Sometimes draws his scars or what he believes they would look like. Dinosaurs or train tracks.

There are no mirrors in the apartment today. She removes the garbage bags from her windows. She shows him photos of steel mills and mannequin factories. A joyful spy, possibly a sister, plays with his shoelaces below the window.

Claire born with fins now removed. She sleeps in the bathtub. She is rarely seen in the window. Sometimes a hand or forehead with half eyes. It is almost impossible to hide from water.

Three Women sometimes Four: Simon.

Girl in Drag stands downstage. The box in the middle not taped shut shutters overlapping and tucked is off stage. Penny Detective sits in the audience in the second row. The audience is mannequins.

Girl in Drag: I'm tired.

Penny Detective: The listeners want to know if it's time to view the body.

Girl in Drag: I require two to three feet of distance to tell my story.

Penny Detective: I understand your request, but it is not useful.

Girl in Drag: You look familiar.

Penny Detective: Possibly.

Girl in Drag: Were you in my refrigerator last night?

Penny Detective: Possibly.

Girl in Drag: You are always there.

Penny Detective: As are you.

Girl in Drag: Always.

Penny Detective: Comforting?

Girl in Drag: Always.

Penny Detective: Disturbing?

Girl in Drag: I have decided that always and never mean the same thing.

Penny Detective: Possibly.

Girl in Drag: You have many names.

Penny Detective: I must have been well-schooled.

Girl in Drag: You must have a good memory.

Penny Detective: I have no memory at all.

Girl in Drag: Then how do you move?

Penny Detective: Very carefully, mostly with my legs.

Girl in Drag looks down at her hands, at him, at her hands, him, her hands, turns hands over and over and over, over and over. Climbs into bed.

Girl in Drag: How do I know if they're accurate?

Back of the neck, unable to fully turn, spreads to shoulders.

Girl in Drag becomes as small as a handshake unable to leave the bed. Squeezes covers between chest and thighs. The wind outside sounds like waves. Maybe Maine. A boat not a bed, old and wooden. There is a chance it will not last the day's weather.

Keep eyes closed.

Beneath boat not bed someone hides with a tape recorder.

The making of a jury. Upon hearing bad news, an elite memory squad is hired, but closeness has its own legs.

The smell of a cluttered kitchen faces east.
She remembers a wraparound porch.
It is Maine.

Just stay in bed.

Children chase each other in the front yard.

In a lot of saying, much is said. This red wine is fantastic.

She brushes a mosquito from her knee.
The cat jumps onto the railing.
There is laughter in the spoons.

More force is possible with a table. A landscape is not nervous.

Girl in Drag places occupations in a jar, tears pieces of masking tape, and covers jar. Overlapping each torn-edge-tape-piece, she leaves a viewing space on the side.

An open-lid-top-view and a side view will provide different results.

Stains the tape with brown shoe polish, creating a self-antique. She cuts a hole in the lid. Inserts a wire that connects to other wires, other jars, other occupations.

Possibly more than one person is located here. A system of wired containers in which communication is available.

She lines up the jars on the floor. Sits in front of them. Listens.

A study of what is left behind.

Boy with many Occupations shines a spotlight on each witness.

Witness 1: He carried around a wooden leg, stories of injury. From what I heard, she opened the door and he promised to leave. He whispered in her ear to get her down from the kitchen counter. The wooden leg began to multiply not just legs but other dangerous collections. It ended. She walked into the room. He saw her.

Witness 2: He said I feel Norman when he was down and couldn't get out. He was Norman most of the time. She started to say Norman too and growled about the room. Even their daughter said it and bent her fingers monster-like. They called her Sam, or Maud when they wrote it. No one remembered the full name. Relatives went about with three versions: they had a daughter, their daughter died at a young age, or they never had a daughter.

Witness 3: Two spines walked into a bar one curved one straight. Two spines walked into a bar one curved one straight. Two spines walked into a bar one curved one straight.

Witness 4: He brought a device to show off or to examine. They tested filters. They all knew we would pick red first, but they played this game anyways. From what I heard, she laughed. He said how are you? A little Norman. He said yes, you should talk to my sister. What are you doing? He said late and mother is trying. They laughed when I said my daughter. He said I have not changed yet. I still have some of your clothes.

Witness 5: I heard he broke in and she let him stay. The apartment all-lights-on was filled with mannequin parts. They said you could hear them at all times, more noticeable at night. It began in a funeral home.

Three Women sometimes Four: Miss Chipped with the language revolver and a bag full of image cookies in the library scene.

Ancestor on the News (*off stage*): Two or more players may occupy the same dot.

A one-bedroom apartment, second floor, all lights on, 5 a.m. In the living room.

Boy with many Occupations: When does your flight leave?

Girl in Drag: Delayed.

Boy with many Occupations: Is that a time?

Girl in Drag: That's what I was told.

Boy with many Occupations: What are you reading?

Girl in Drag: *Airplanes for Charlie.*

Boy with many Occupations: What's the story?

Girl in Drag: It's about a first-round-out spelling bee contestant, a 30-year-old underdog, and their unlikely relationship.

Boy with many Occupations: How is it?

Girl in Drag: Haven't started.

Boy with many Occupations: Your bookmark is in the middle.

Girl in Drag: Sometimes I don't know how to explain it.

In the hallway.

Boy with many Occupations: Is there a place I can rest my head?

Girl in Drag: Are you looking for safety?

Boy with many Occupations: Today, yes.

Girl in Drag: Do I know you?

Boy with many Occupations: You've known me for years.

Girl in Drag: I just met you a minute ago.

Boy with many Occupations: You're suddenly uncomfortable now that you call me stranger.

Girl in Drag: You've become stranger; of course, I'm uncomfortable.

In the kitchen.

Girl in Drag: Are you in love with me?

Boy with many Occupations thinks for a minute.

Boy with many Occupations: Ask me again, and I'll answer right away.

Girl in Drag: Are you in love with me?

Boy with many Occupations thinks for two minutes.

Boy with many Occupations: I can't answer that quickly.

Girl in Drag: Have you grown tired?

Boy with many Occupations: At times I've been tired.

Girl in Drag: Will you stay here?

Boy with many Occupations: Your sudden questioning is so endearing.

Girl in Drag: Avoidance of questions with insincere compliments.

Boy with many Occupations: I'm new to this.

In the bathroom.

Girl in Drag: We are supposed to be talking about time-travel.

Boy with many Occupations: Why?

Girl in Drag: Yesterday, Ancestor on the News gave a suspicious look.

Boy with many Occupations: When one moves too quickly, there is a chance of misreading.

Girl in Drag: I have identified the location of the problem.

Boy with many Occupations: In the shoulders.

Girl in Drag: How did you know?

Boy with many Occupations: Ancestor on the News.

Girl in Drag: Ancestor is quite upsetting.

Boy with many Occupations: And helpful.

Into the closet.

Girl in Drag: But what is the problem?

Boy with many Occupations: The siblings?

Girl in Drag: I used to think so.

Boy with many Occupations: Stage fright when crossing a large intersection?

Girl in Drag: Possibly.

Boy with many Occupations: Dirty dishes?

Girl in Drag: Now you make fun of me.

Boy with many Occupations: Sometimes I let you sleep in.

Girl in Drag: Sometimes I pretend to be sleeping.

Boy with many Occupations: This is quite upsetting.

Girl in Drag: And helpful.

In the bedroom.

Girl in Drag: Am I asking too many questions?

Boy with many Occupations: Yes, and not enough.

Boy with many Occupations turns off bedroom light. Bedroom into kitchen. Girl in Drag and Boy with many Occupations are sleeping in bed. Girl in Drag gets up and goes into the kitchen. She opens the refrigerator door and kneels down, searching for something to eat. The refrigerator is filled with only condiments and a television on the first shelf. Television turns on, and Ancestor on the News appears on it. She sees Ancestor on the television and lights a cigarette. Girl in Drag speaks to Ancestor on the television in a proper English dialect.

Girl in Drag: Unfortunate.

Ancestor on the News: Quiet, he will hear you.

Girl in Drag: The bottles on the counter are empty.

Ancestor on the News: What are you looking for?

Girl in Drag: No loud questions.

Ancestor on the News: Waiting.

Girl in Drag: It goes familiar then far.

Ancestor on the News: A 12-year-old from Indiana committed suicide after losing local spelling bee. A community in shock. A neighbor was heard to remark, a shy girl, didn't say much, but her drawings of animals were exceptional. The local dentist said they seemed like a normal family; you just don't think something like this can happen in your neighborhood.

Girl in Drag: Next time I shall bring a coat.

Girl in Drag closes the refrigerator door, stands there smoking. Lights out in kitchen for a minute. Lights up, Girl in Drag is in the same place. She turns on the kitchen faucet to put out the cigarette. She opens the refrigerator door, sits down, and lights a cigarette.

Girl in Drag: Unfortunate.

Ancestor on the News: Have you misplaced something?

Girl in Drag: Have you seen my spunk?

Ancestor on the News: She was last seen in puffy sleeves near train tracks.

Girl in Drag: I know the ducks on the front lawn, but what's the idea?

Ancestor on the News: I notice the way you sit.

Girl in Drag: A slump in the shoulders.

Ancestor on the News: There is never a clean story.

Girl in Drag: What about expectation?

Ancestor on the News: Spelling bee first-round-out not charmed. There was a fall. All the papers covered it. She was not one to speak first or second. This was not a zipper. The community thought to say but instead understated and obvious. Comments only sent them the sound of pulling. There was talk in a car. Unrecorded.

Girl in Drag: You try to sit bright. I adore you.

Girl in Drag closes the refrigerator door. Lights out in kitchen for a minute. Lights up, Girl in Drag is in the same place. She turns on the faucet to put out the cigarette. She opens the refrigerator door and sits down. She holds a cigarette that she never lights.

Girl in Drag: Unfortunate.

Ancestor on the News: I have never heard you talk so much.

Girl in Drag: Is this being recorded?

Ancestor on the News: Now I recognize you.

Girl in Drag: What about rooms, assembly lines, and things that have wings?

Ancestor on the News: You are moving too fast.

Girl in Drag: I want to build a case for the sound in the next room.

Ancestor on the News: Girl known as lower case. The papers said no note was found. Beneath bed not boat there was a note that read…

Girl in Drag: Speak. Sound in head. Is that allowed? I speak sometimes. You hurt me when you walk through me. There is a long staircase of a seamstress with ready caramels. I don't think her hair is real, but her stairs are tempting. No more than two steps. Shit, why am I not braver?

Girl in Drag takes out the shelves in the refrigerator and the television. She enters the refrigerator and closes the door. The television, now on the kitchen floor, is still on. Ancestor on the News lights a cigarette and turns around to reveal a refrigerator. Opens it. There is a television on the first shelf. Ancestor turns on the television, and Girl in Drag appears on it. Lights out.

Act II:
The Making of a Jury

The memory is set in winter near water.
It is filmed through a red filter.
The old house mixes with new sounds.

Girl in Drag places nicknames out of hand or carried away.

There is no negotiation of armrest.

She thinks of the word gradual, its way of being sneaky.

Back of the knee, skin tends to gather. How compelling is her furniture arrangement. When not allowed to go upstairs, children create stories. Cardboard and blankets. The seamstress' husband is always upstairs. In bed she wishes she knew more about the body inside, salt in the bloodstream, finicky eaters, and how to escape.

Before she notices, she is in another room.

A lower level of the Always Room, a dislocation of color. Girl in Drag gets a job in retail.

Name six cosmetic solutions for binging.

She becomes addicted to pulling out her teeth. She drives in circles without teeth in a shopping cart.

Tear at each advance until she is lower case. The stain of a dandelion.

A thigh tries to escape a leather booth.

The removal of teeth is associated with memory loss and obsessive cleaning.

Depressed Refrigerator tries to open fake doors in the dressing room.

Character becomes question. Is sitting on an egg levelheaded? There is talk, usually a couple feet away. Whispering is creepy.

Girl in Drag thinks about leaving.

Depressed Refrigerator loses her legs. Escape mid-thigh, she does not scream. To avoid scar-watching, Girl in Drag places two buckets on her stumps. Girl in Drag carries her piggy-back-style down the street. They chase. The legs move with confidence and avoid obstacles such as small dogs and parking meters.

Depressed Refrigerator has never seen her legs move like this.

The legs arrive at O'Hare International Airport, lock themselves in an airplane, and dangle in a window seat. Drag and Fridge are lost in the airport. The legs fall asleep. They dream of a backyard with other legs in a plastic pool, swing then monkey bar, robber to someone's cop. The legs dream for three days until local law enforcement apprehends them and returns them to the Always Room, where Doctor Clubhouse reattaches them.

Three Women sometimes Four: Around this time or this gives rise to the popularity of insects. They are on everything: necklaces, telephone poles, and shoulders. All is unseen or small. Corner of the eye, did you see that? Well, you will.

No stage directions available at this time.

The Teeth I Lost when I was Four: How long have you been down here?

Depressed Refrigerator: One foot in at all times.

The Teeth I Lost when I was Four: Is someone pacing in the upstairs bedroom?

Depressed Refrigerator: That is someone else's.

The Teeth I Lost when I was Four: Are you letting them know how dark it is here?

Depressed Refrigerator: The crawl space of an estranged relative.

The Teeth I Lost when I was Four: Tell them what it smells like here.

The Teeth I Lost when I was Four: Are you still here?

The Teeth I Lost when I was Four: Where did you just go?

The Teeth I Lost when I was Four: Are you okay?

Depressed Refrigerator: I think S is red, and there's nothing I can do about it.

Girl in Drag performs an act of chasing.

The moment the room becomes the bottom of a boat. Reset the counter. Begin as usual. Line stomach with clay and feathers. Pick out costumes to match landscape. Flash armpit. Towards the middle, things have an option. Things are purchased or fastened. A piece of family secret is let out twice a year.

Girl in Drag places herself or is trapped underneath a familiar boat. She stays there for two days to two years, water in the nose.

She remembers space museum,
Chicago, in line for simulation ride.
Everything is round.

Pass group photo, remember explosion and the teacher with the curly hair. Surfacing does not mean escape hatch or marathon. This leads to resetting the counter. Circle a date. Chase a photograph of a contestant, which is her. As a child her eyes were indeed bigger than her stomach. Go swimming with t-shirt on.

Girl in Drag enters warm climate, possible vacation destination. She walks into a general store, side of the road. Joints move backwards at elbows and knees, slowly of customers. Much is dust, shelves and the outlines of bodies.

Is that the Depressed Refrigerator in the last aisle concealing something, magnets or fabric?

Fridge appears to be eating magnets or fabric. A closer look, no one is there.

Remember to ask her later.

Are you okay asks the man behind the counter, the woman at work, the woman in the bathroom, and the man at the bar.

Yes, yes, just trying to make a phone call. Can't remember the number or have no control over my fingers.

Boy with many Occupations shines a spotlight on each witness.

Witness 1: The way the girl said across the street, made her think it was not directly across. There was a general store, a tumbleweed with sunglasses on the front porch. He reclaimed his cigarette from the ashtray and pointed at the door. Inside was a coat rack, and she entered. A child again. Circled by spaces fitted for shoulders, she pulled on the coats, hung for a moment, fell onto the sales floor, saw her mother, and said I think I'm going to die.

Witness 2: They said he was never the same after, in the bathroom with a seashell against his ear. Many were uncles, steel and water. They said she was never any trouble, not even when older. The children were left on the front porch. His spontaneity was endearing at parties. She was not well known for her promptness.

Witness 3: She believed in leaving to-do lists around the house even days after the tasks were completed just in case she died. Then people would find the lists and say she was organized and efficient.

Witness 4: The mother asked, every time she visited, do you ever play that thing, referring to the piano, and have you met any of your neighbors? She thought if God created us then who created God; she thought she was onto something. The children were kissed goodnight. He waited in a temper. She was inconsolable when evenings came to an end.

Witness 5: A child again. She entered a general store with the word *joyful*. She bought a postcard of where land meets water. The weather was unusually cold that week. The smell of heat in the store made one feel like Christmas was coming. It was April and music played.

Three Women sometimes Four: An empty room says what?

At the end of the bar, there is a loose tooth on the left side of the mouth.

Wiggle it back and forth. Remove easily without pain then place on bar with other teeth. No concern.

On the right side of the mouth, there are three teeth missing. There is an investigation of the empty space with the tongue or a memory tool. It is 3:14 a.m., soft tissue. No sounds at this time.

They will be remembered later.

Stop and start again to make sure the teeth are really missing. Pick up missing teeth and eat them easily until smaller pieces, until gone.

The mouth is happily surprised at its success.

Nervousness is the need to speed up or slow down. Feel the exposed gums. Look around.

Mouth wonders what happened to its teeth.

Crawl on the floor searching, the sound of pulling.

Package Liquor Bar. The metal leg catches the light from the jukebox. One can see two springs tucked into tiny black shoes. Depressed Refrigerator pulls at her genes.

Memory affects perception.

> There is a card game, a boat, and secrets.
> There is a leave.

Girl in Drag enters all wet, looks for joyful.

> Shh, do not bring it up.

The legs have been gone for six months. Fridge looks at the door, neighborhood couple not legs.

The moment of telling affects the memory told.

> There is a mention of lost souls, running,
> no luggage, and others just like.

The legs enter in the usual disguise: hat, glasses, and mustache. They sit at the front of the bar.

Is that a memory or a film, that sense of a net?

> They tell their secrets.
> A change, escape is lost.
> Heavy winds.

The legs walk toward the door. Fridge looks up.

Three Women sometimes Four: It's the realization of teeth and bathroom mirrors that keep the barstools warm.

The following scenes are displayed on the screen upstage. The Cast of Laughables are in the audience, watching. Any movement or dialogue by the Cast of Laughables as audience should be improvised, changing each time it is performed.

FADE IN:

INT. CHICAGO BAR - NIGHT

GIRL IN DRAG smokes a Parliament Light and drinks an Absolut Martini, dirty, extra blue cheese olives. DEPRESSED REFRIGERATOR drinks gin, well gin not name brand, and tonic with a small lime wedge. She wishes she was drinking a Margarita or a Long Island, something a little more festive. It is 11:36 p.m. on a Thursday, summer.

>GIRL IN DRAG
>It's too early for fireworks.

>DEPRESSED REFRIGERATOR
>Last night I caught myself listening to my neighbor's fight.

A jazz band starts to play, making the sound of talk and clanking glasses more noticeable.

>GIRL IN DRAG
>Caught yourself?

                    DEPRESSED REFRIGERATOR
               Apparently, I've been doing this for months.
               I realized this after a phone message from
               my mother stating that she wants to travel,
               maybe France, Greece, or Las Vegas. My
               father's obsession with saving newspapers,
               free samples, and stealing restaurant
               glassware has finally taken its toll on her.

THE TEETH I LOST WHEN I WAS FOUR enters the bar. Sits in a corner booth, appears to be waiting for someone. Orders a glass of Shiraz.

                         GIRL IN DRAG
               I once stole my mother's birth control
               pills to get attention. I got a brother.

The jazz band throws hearing aids into the crowd while still playing a tune BILLIE HOLIDAY used to sing. A voice is heard from the back of the bar.

                         BILLIE HOLIDAY (O.S.)
               If you're going to do a foxtrot, do a
               foxtrot.

INT. COLORADO BAR - NIGHT

> GIRL IN DRAG
> I'm thinking of leaving.

> DEPRESSED REFRIGERATOR
> I'm occasionally bulimic.

> GIRL IN DRAG
> This night is going to end, isn't it?

> DEPRESSED REFRIGERATOR
> Most likely...does that upset you?

> GIRL IN DRAG
> It ending or not ending?

> DEPRESSED REFRIGERATOR
> Either.

> GIRL IN DRAG
> I'm not sure.

INT. CHICAGO OR NEW YORK BAR - NIGHT

> GIRL IN DRAG
> (to bartender)
> ...and then the third time my arm fell out...

> DEPRESSED REFRIGERATOR
> Not the dislocation of your arm story again.

> GIRL IN DRAG
> I know, I'm sick of hearing it too. I keep telling the same story over and over again. I'm thinking of adding some new details, try to tell it in a different way. Maybe add some characters.

> DEPRESSED REFRIGERATOR
> What about lying? It's really not hard; it just takes practice.

> GIRL IN DRAG
> No, what's upsetting is that I don't think I could even pass a lie detector. With my shaky nerves, the machine would go spastic.

> DEPRESSED REFRIGERATOR
> Sometimes it takes the machine days to find my pulse.

INT. NEW YORK BAR - NIGHT

Girl in Drag and Depressed Refrigerator sit in a round booth. The table is littered with glasses, photos, and things that one keeps in one's pockets such as lighters and keys. Drag has a spindle sticking out of her head. There is a red ribbon tied in a bow around the spindle. Fridge's hair is pulled back in a loosely tied ponytail.

          DEPRESSED REFRIGERATOR
You know there's a spindle sticking out of your head.

          GIRL IN DRAG
A what?

          DEPRESSED REFRIGERATOR
A spindle, a sharp silver stand used for stacking receipts or notes of some sort by puncturing a hole through them.

          GIRL IN DRAG
Oh yeah, sometimes I forget.

          DEPRESSED REFRIGERATOR
Did you see the news today about the spelling bee contestant?

          GIRL IN DRAG
No, must not have been paying attention.

          DEPRESSED REFRIGERATOR
No one knows how it started. They said there was no kidnapping or suicide.

GIRL IN DRAG
It's been almost eighteen years.

Close-up shot of the spindle.

DEPRESSED REFRIGERATOR
What's with the ribbon on it?

GIRL IN DRAG
I'm trying to draw attention away from the spindle.

DEPRESSED REFRIGERATOR
I think it's a cover up. She went to stay with her grandparents or study abroad. There was some kind of move. When the neighbors didn't see her anymore, one person said one thing then another. Relatives can't be reached for comments.

GIRL IN DRAG
It got out of hand.

DEPRESSED REFRIGERATOR
(points to spindle)
Why don't you remove it?

GIRL IN DRAG
Then what would I replace it with?

ESSENTIAL TREMOR enters the bar, orders a shot of Jack, and tells a joke. No one laughs. Essential Tremor laughs loudly, takes the shot, and leaves.

DEPRESSED REFRIGERATOR
You do keep it very clean.

GIRL IN DRAG
Thanks.

INT. SPLIT SCREEN – INDOOR SWIMMING POOL AND
WATERSLIDE TUBE – CITY LOCATION UNKNOWN – DAY

Girl in Drag sits in a drained indoor swimming pool. Depressed Refrigerator is stuck in a waterslide tube. Two phones are located, one on the wall of the pool and one in the tube. They talk by phone.

> DEPRESSED REFRIGERATOR
> I seem to be stuck in some sort of tube.

> GIRL IN DRAG
> Like a waterslide, the enclosed part?

> DEPRESSED REFRIGERATOR
> It appears so.

> GIRL IN DRAG
> It's happened to me before.

> DEPRESSED REFRIGERATOR
> How did you get out?

> GIRL IN DRAG
> I don't remember.

> DEPRESSED REFRIGERATOR
> Where are you?

INT. SPLIT SCREEN – PRESENT DAY – WATERSLIDE TUBE –
AND FLASHBACK – INDIANA 1940

Depressed Refrigerator sits on the phone, waiting for a response from the question she just asked. RED GIRL runs into the kitchen to find her mother, PURPLE WOMAN.

                    RED GIRL
Now, Mom, don't get mad, but Dad sold more dishes
for whiskey today.

                    PURPLE WOMAN
Let's go. Get your coat. We're going to the picture
show.

END FLASHBACK.

INT. SPLIT SCREEN – INDOOR SWIMMING POOL AND
WATERSLIDE TUBE - DAY

                    GIRL IN DRAG AS RED GIRL

The Garden Show on Main Street gave you dishes when you bought film tickets. He looked like Clark Gable. She tried to sober him up. She took him to the picture show.

                    DEPRESSED REFRIGERATOR

What? Where are you?

                    GIRL IN DRAG

A drained indoor swimming pool, the deep end.

                    DEPRESSED REFRIGERTOR

I should try to get out of this.

                    GIRL IN DRAG

I think I found a way.

FADE OUT.

Act III:
Station 30:
An Emergency Post

Girl in Drag goes through boxes, drawers, and closets at Station 30.

The lock slipped. Photographs of small incisions. Badge on desk read Paper Father, an assumed nickname. Station 30: An Emergency Post was abandoned before we arrived. The Station charted the fastest horse of 1974. Mannequins were interrogated in the backroom. Orange couch, vinyl in the basement, tear in middle cushion duct taped, and cardboard dividers for a sense of. Upstairs someone was in a box being observed. Three decks of cards: 1. Las Vegas, 2. naked Marilyn, and 3. standard red backing. Bottom left drawer, possible allies. This was a lucky hand or a loose tooth. Did he ask if it was bleeding? More sinister than remembered by a bartender in Chicago. Less apple than ice box.

She always wanted a chair by a window. She said you only meet six types of people in life. Expectation was located in the shoulders. The boys at Station 30 tasted like gravel, descendants of carnival, machinery under their nails. One day no one came back. They forgot to retrieve boots. A black cat stood in the doorway, camera slung.

From the point of view of the building, there are three kinds of leaving:

1. Pack everything, someone else moves in.
2. Demolish and rebuild.
3. Abandon, a kind of preserving with eventual weathering.

Building not as location, building as emotional. The room knew the history of rope and exposed pipes in the basement. They left. The rope made its last appearance upstairs.

Water occupied bone. A certain amount was passed. A collection of 45s, space heater right corner, toilet seat wracked. He left the photographs (the woman with her eyes closed) on a day that didn't require an iron and polish. Your real name wasn't given yet. We passed by a steel mill town, no slower.

The one with the mustache wasn't there. He went over to the Baker Street house.

The pharmacist repeated everything twice. She wasn't hungry. She cried.

Didn't touch the gun. Under the strap. This deserved a hair ribbon.

Were they twins?

No.

Could the girl speak?

They were told to play outside.

After, the idea of the detective was placed in an empty olive jar in the cabinet above the stove behind the honey.

Three Women sometimes Four: Tremor is the involuntary rhythmic oscillation of reciprocally innervated antagonistic muscle groups causing movement of a body part about a fixed plane in space.

One of the Paper Fathers sits on a bench, appears to be waiting. He clutches the box in the middle not taped shut shutters overlapping and tucked in his hands. Essential Tremor enters stage right, crosses Paper Father's path, and sits next to him. Paper Father does not seem to notice Essential Tremor.

Essential Tremor: Do you remember me?

Paper Father: You used to be a little boy.

Essential Tremor: I suppose I grew.

Paper Father: I don't know you.

Essential Tremor: What are you waiting for?

Paper Father: An elephant.

Essential Tremor: Here?

Paper Father: The investors told me to wait here.

Essential Tremor: What investors?

Paper Father: The ones on the news.

Essential Tremor: What is the elephant for?

Paper Father: A business venture.

Essential Tremor: They invest in elephants?

Paper Father: In ideas. I'm not sure what's next.

Essential Tremor: I'm in the middle of a case.

Paper Father: We have something in common.

Essential Tremor: You remember?

Paper Father: I remember a ghost t-shirt and a moving van. Everything else could be a film I once saw.

Essential Tremor: What's in the box?

Paper Father looks at Essential Tremor for the first time in the scene.

Paper Father: Oh, I didn't see you sitting there. Are you waiting for the Clark Street bus too? It's running late.

Paper Father and Essential Tremor stare into the audience. No one moves for a moment. Paper Father hands Essential Tremor the box in the middle not taped shut shutters overlapping and tucked. Essential Tremor takes the box, gets up, and exits stage left. Paper Father continues to wait.

Girl in Drag watches a commercial for the Recording Room.

Pilot from a Dream: And if Chicago is your home, welcome back.

Winter. Low light. Possible candles. Midwest bar. The holidays. Garland over bottles. Heater smell. Blue and yellow. They were trying harder to make the relationship work. To save things she suggested: buying a dog, a trip longer than four days (maybe two weeks), or something erotic. A profile, then stare into camera. The other profile, the shy one now passing by east coast windows. The Christmas decorations in that bar tell her. I have been at this too long. She said I used to be on time until I moved east. My mother is never on time. So I'm either growing into this city or my mother. Driving in the Midwest, years earlier. Dirty snow. Garland again. Old movie theater. Glitter on gray. Back seat. Train car graffiti. Boarded windows. Gravel. Like East Chicago. A car ride to a holiday. Snow in traffic pushed to the color of a steel mill town. Christmas decorations at intersections. Thirty minutes.

Girl in Drag takes a seat in the Recording Room.

During the 1990s, some of the O'Hare International Airport temporary Terminal 4 furniture was donated to a little-known business called the Recording Room, run by one Doctor Clubhouse. It was located in an abandoned mannequin factory, past down from generation to generation. The factory folded after what was known as the Butternut Street incident. Mannequins and mannequin parts remained. The chairs were in sets of threes and fours, armrest included. Teal and burgundy. Stand-up ashtrays that had not been cleaned in some time. A black and white TV on wheels was always on (helped them sleep at night). Clients sat with headphones and listened to their memories in an effort to, a study of. Shh, the listeners could not tell. The headphones backed away slowly, unnoticed.

Girl in Drag puts on headphones. The following memories are displayed on the screen upstage.

They slid the plastic pool into the back seat of the car, upright. It fit, curved over child. All aquatic. She was afraid. There was nowhere to move or look out. This was the beginning of something. The kids asked if she could turn into anything right now what it would be. She said a glass of orange juice. They laughed, and she wished she said tiger. I saw your son-in-law playing cards on the table with the newspaper design. They made up stories, rules of travel: avoid the jester, make it to the castle, a large hat or sewing machine along the way. Ma'am, we found your husband. In the bathtub, he placed his elbow near the drain. The elbow sported a scab, an earlier race with sibling. Large carnival wire. It was her chin. The stitches looked like a beard growing. The lie or the drain carried the injury away like water. Ma'am, we found your husband. In dreams when she needed to run from something she dropped to all fours, animal-like, or she beat her arms furiously and took off flying or she put her hands in the shape of a gun and made the sound of a shot. This seemed to work when she repeated it's all true.

Boy with many Occupations turns on the projector. Witnesses appear on the screen upstage at a younger age.

Witness 1: There was a hammock and a wooden porch added five years after arrival, and a creek in the backyard. She named six escape routes. A plastic pool was emptied. Left its imprint, flat grass. Children pretended to be mechanics.

Witness 2: She was in a car. It was after eleven. There was a Hello Kitty in the upstairs bedroom window. Lily Finn's grandfather placed chairs in front of the doors at night. Black vinyl kitchen chair, stuck to your thighs, was at the side door. One of two living room chairs, peach covered in plastic, at front door. Her sleep was compared to a log. She faced certain ways to avoid nightmares. She was afraid of the zebra blanket.

Witness 3: Black and white photos, wigs, nicknames, political buttons, water bugs, a deck of naked Marilyn Monroe playing cards, furs, colors, shoeboxes with nothing in them, a gun, costume jewelry, hard candy, multiplication tables, Saint Christopher, safety pins, Kermit and Lincoln's head, Christmas decorations, two fifth place science projects, a limited edition Pepsi can, dishwashing liquid and the solar system, rope, Styrofoam hat, magnets, adoption papers, 99 Red Balloons, and a cherished family pet named Spunky.

Witness 4: Lake Michigan, corner of bike path just north of Oak Street Beach, a view of a curve and a lighthouse were points of safety. A boat called Mi Shadow pulled out of the East Chicago Harbor around seven this morning. The grandfather did not have a tattoo of a Polish eagle on his chest instead a scar not a gunshot wound from his mother-in-law but from World War II, purple hearts. A banner tattoo on his left shoulder read Mother.

Witness 5: A long-distance runner three times a week, a bridge, frozen eyelashes, there was a horse. Was it the holidays? Painted like a snow village. Mercy Bee securely held piano books. There was a jump, or was it summer? Willow trees as transportation, as weapons. They woke up and saw ducks on the front lawn.

Three Women sometimes Four (*off stage*): Uncle.

Mill Gate Inn. The following memory is displayed on the screen upstage.

He got a room.

What did he use it for?

He moved the furniture, stood back, looked, he moved furniture.

How often?

He always paid on time.

Was he alone?

Most of the time, sometimes a daughter, sometimes three kids, sometimes someone that looked like him might have been him, maybe a relative.

Why?

Rather rearranged, lit a cigarette, made a drink, stood, looked in the mirror, sat, crossed legs, sipped, then flushed the cigarette down the toilet, washed ashtray in bathroom sink, the glass too, dried, and took out any garbage. In the morning, woke the kids (if kids), always gave the boy the front seat. Compulsiveness needed things to arrive in smaller packages and/or a bad memory. I knew of his father too. The family visited the cemetery across the street, set up a picnic, and spent the afternoon.

Visited?

That's what they did back then. Eventually some of them made their way over to the bar. Sometimes they brought the boy, quiet, played Walkin' after Midnight on the jukebox.

A purple room. The following memory is displayed on the screen upstage.

Two beds divided by tall dresser, above each bed oval frame, flowers in vase. Woman slept in right bed near door. Woman was helped into bed, out of bed. Small girl slept in left bed near window, length of bed. Woman in bed called out in middle of night. Teeth were on long dresser on opposite wall. Woman in bed called out daughter's name. In night, small girl listened to train horns. Woman in bed called daughter's name in night. Train horns woke up small girl, covered feet. Woman was helped out of bed, into bed. In middle of night, woman called daughter's name. Woman was turned in bed. Small girl turned from window to avoid nightmares, ended up in hallway. Small girl was carried back to bed. Woman fell in hallway, was carried back to bed in middle of night. Woman called for water. Small girl missed mouth; water rolled down cheek. Small girl called for help. In middle of night, woman in bed called out.

A yellow and red landscape. The following dream is displayed on the screen upstage.

Pilot crashed plane in cornfield in Indiana. Engine gave out. Pilot was hospitalized and promised never to eat corn again. Next year, pilot crashed plane in cornfield in Indiana near sign that said Private Property No Trespassing in red letters. Engine trouble again. Pilot was hospitalized and promised never to wear color red again. Following year, pilot crashed plane for third time in Indiana cornfield near red sign that said Private Property No Trespassing just past pond with ducks. Pilot was hospitalized and thought about water and birds, corn, red, water and birds. Nurse suggested engine repair. Pilot's heart moved into stomach and refused to leave.

Three Paper Fathers and Boy with many Occupations enter stage left and walk across the stage. Their dialogue is spoken as they cross the stage.

Paper Fathers: We believe we are based on real people.

Boy with many Occupations: I forgot my line.

Three Paper Fathers pull out pieces of paper from their back pockets.

Paper Fathers: It says, you say by a show of hands, I see what you mean.

Boy with many Occupations: I would never say that.

Paper Fathers: We don't think these are our lines.

They exit stage right.

Penny Detective presents this report.

Red was back for the reason; she did not remember it. She referred to it as polite, joy ruffled over breakfast. Too tired to remember the lesson if one was given. She handled it so well they said. Double shot of, holiday shopping was in full swing. Impressed or disgusted, itch gained strength. Talk became effort. Grandfather clock was so disappointed. The boat wore initials of each available surprise. A pear was a nice place to end a year. Hopeful wore a badge that was often misplaced. Talk of this produced a gag. How one returned to places of comfort only to realize that comfort had gained confidence and left for Europe. She paused then vacuumed up red. Guest never knew. They enjoyed their wine and conversation. When one was refused, takeout was ordered. Substitutions were unaware at first by definition. Stains were rewarded. Cruel balloon found music under a pillow. In private she bit a chicken and justified it with a trial. Shyness created the most elaborate escapes.

Ancestor on the News presents this report.

An extra in North by Northwest, the tree before the tree visible. 99 Red Balloons carried a letter with monster truck stickers on it. Case memory: a moment existing past the moment contained in a new or different form. Example, her life as a single mother contained in an armchair by a window. What was he doing down there in the basement so long? A brother went back and brought Anna Banana to the states. A sister worked in the steel mills. A mother-in-law gave bread and thought they were happy, grateful. She stayed with him. On the line she made fifth wheels, picture a horseshoe for trucks. They said one would be locked up if his country believed in. A third child would. He forgot to ask about the price of postage.

A hallway, a wooden door, and a sense of travel.

She stopped reading (not sure how they got the body out of) the room. Over the years, they took the same picture, haircuts as well. A lot of driving reminded us of what we had been avoiding. At some point it was time to take the side of an older sibling, least like. In the film the pawnbroker slammed his hand through the spindle to save his soul. She was overwhelmed by feet-over-metal-grids, memories without teeth, and indoor swimming pools. Didn't remember when it started, the collections, the repetitions. Mannequin parts appeared. They put them in boxes. More legs, more arms so they bought more boxes. Finally, the room was locked up. For years, the phone did not ring. She picked it up and said doctor, doctor.

Two mannequins sit at a table. Agreeable Utensil and Even Number of Sentences stand behind each mannequin. They hold a script; they speak for the mannequins. The mannequins play cards, six different card games at once. Agreeable Utensil and Even Number of Sentences move the cards for them.

Even Number of Sentences: These things never start on time.

Agreeable Utensil: Is this being recorded?

Even Number of Sentences: Yes.

Agreeable Utensil: Does she leave?

Even Number of Sentences: No, it's your turn to deal.

Agreeable Utensil: Oh, sorry.

Even Number of Sentences: Yes.

Agreeable Utensil: When?

Even Number of Sentences: The script says she places her hand on the door knob.

Under Agreeable Utensil's (mannequin's) chair is the box in the middle not taped shut shutters overlapping and tucked. Agreeable Utensil puts the box on the table. They continue to play.

The following scene is performed on stage and projected on screen from a different angle. Girl in Drag walks into a bar or an attic. Slanted walls for oversized paintings. She lifts a glass with the right hand, the stronger one. Essential Tremor is across the room. Walks over and hands her twenty pages of a script. Girl in Drag looks away. No windows in this room. The light is soft

no say rose, say this room is a room I remember as a child of a room I don't remember. This chandelier is not in the remembering. The chandelier is before the children and after Greece.

Girl in Drag alternates her hands back and forth in front of her face, a push and a pull.

Vertigo is two viewing-spaces seen at the same time.

She begins to read the script. Draws back her shoulders. From her pocket she removes a postcard of where land meets water and writes the possibility of red is always present. Curtain.

Epilogue

Time hunches over. A kitchen table holds so much water. There is no shortage of potatoes in the basement. The first action is a heart attack. Water runs down orange flowered wallpaper. The flowers grow until alive, until possible. From this we know one is much loved. A timepiece is found with its mouth open. Tools are located: a crossword puzzle for memory, the sense of a room not yet built, and a hiding place for baby teeth. When things become heard (become uncertain), characters are introduced. They arrive at night without a full script. To arrive at night in a new town versus to arrive in the day, at night allows you to arrive twice. Much is still unseen. Waking up to arrive again and say the morning brings. It is morning in a new town.

STEFANIA IRENE MARTHAKIS was born in Northwest Indiana just outside of Chicago. Stefania holds a BA in Poetry & Theatre from Columbia College Chicago and an MFA in Poetry & Poetics from Naropa University. She interned and volunteered at The Poetry Project and attended The European Graduate School. Stefania is the author of three chapbooks: *The Summer Flood Came Home*, *The Picture Show* (Another New Calligraphy, 2016), and *A Filmmaker's Handbook* (dancing girl press, 2017). Her poems can be found in *Columbia Poetry Review*, *New American Writing*, *Bombay Gin*, *The Recluse*, *Lungfull!*, *Tarpaulin Sky Press*, and *The Brooklyn Rail*, among others. www.simarthakis.com

www.ingramcontent.com/pod-product-compliance
Lightning Source LLC
Chambersburg PA
CBHW011406070526
44577CB00003B/398